THE DYSLEXIC HANDBOOK
Genius Edition

Jimmy Huston

Copyright © 2018 Jimmy Huston

ISBN 978-1-970022-31-5

All rights reserved, including the right to use or reproduce this book or portions thereof in any form whatsoever without written permission from the publisher except in the case of brief quotations embodied in critical articles or reviews.

All images are used under license from Shutterstock.com

Cosworth Publishing
21545 Yucatan Avenue
Woodland Hills CA 91364
www.cosworthpublishing.com

For information regarding permission,
please send an email to office@cosworthpublishing.com.

Dedicated to my wonderful
dyslexic daughters and wife,
Goeriga, Vorenaci and Lnyn,
who have made me so very tired.

-- Love, Jimym

THE END

Just kidding.   Sort of...

As a dyslexic person you see things differently. That's okay.

What is Dyslexia?

Long, long ago, on a remote island in the deepest part of the Sea of Knowledge, there was the grand Kingdom of Dyslexia.

The citizens there were very bright and spoke the same language we speak today -- but they sometimes spelled words differently. (And nobody cared.)

The exact location of the Kingdom of Dyslexia is lost to us because -- well, travelers from there tended to get lost a lot.

Today, their descendants are found throughout the modern world and are widely known for their intelligence and creativity. And they still spell things in odd ways.

Or maybe not.

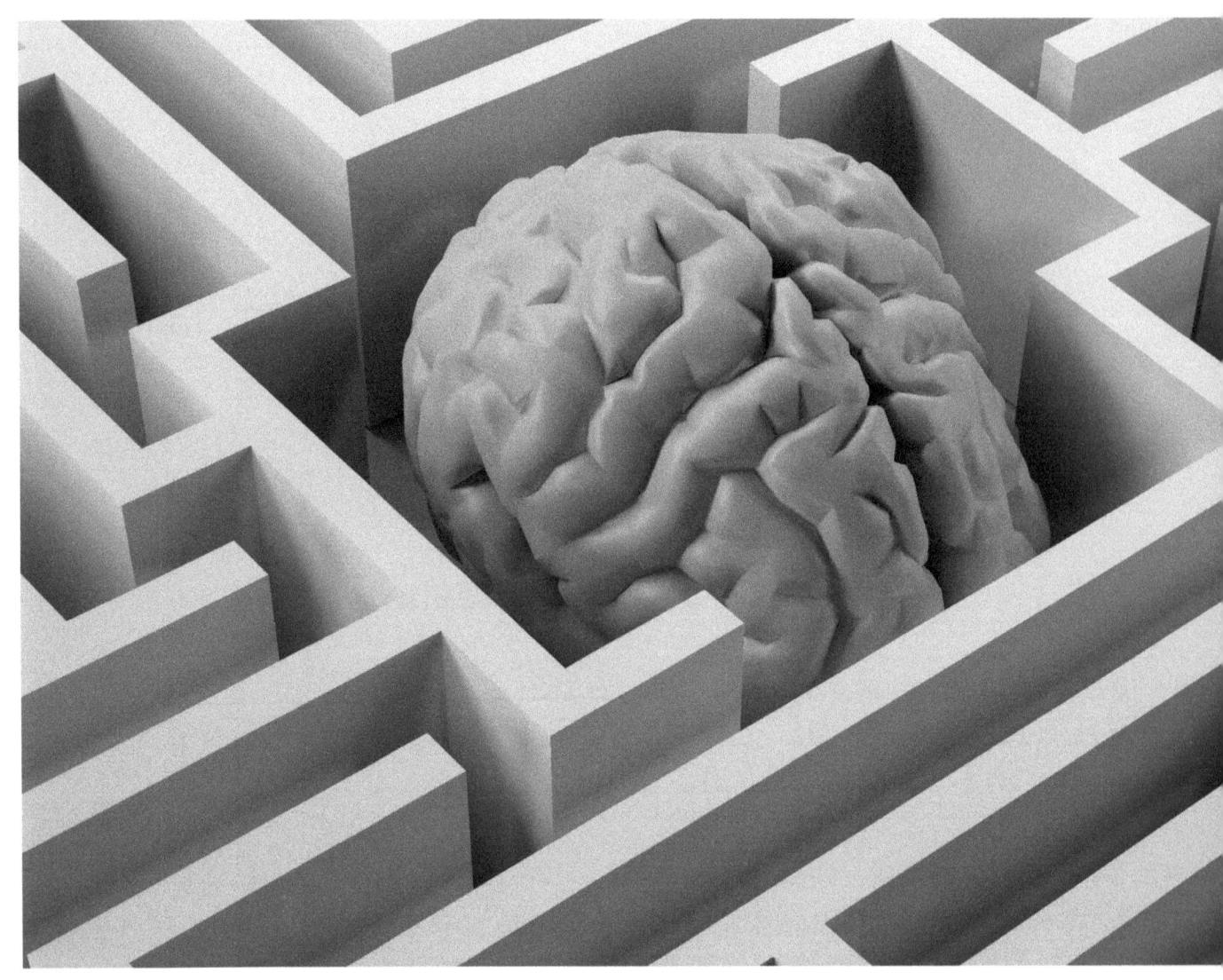

So, what is dyslexia really?

You already know how it feels, but how do you explain it to other people?

Well, dyslexia is different things to different people. It affects how some people process the things they see, or how they understand what they're hearing. It affects how some people think about things and how they express those thoughts. Basically it's a problem with thinking in a straight line, as if thoughts sometimes go round

and round in your brain. They get lost, or they sometimes go to the wrong place. Things get mixed up.

At its core, dyslexia is a difficulty in matching letters to the sounds they represent. There are more clinical and scientific explanations, but they can be hard to follow and depend on who you're listening to. Even doctors say different things about dyslexia. All you really need to know is that you're going to be okay.

Hold your head up.

There's nothing to be ashamed of.

Tired of being teased?

Keep smiling. Keep working.

It does **NOT** mean you're dumb.

You're gonna do great. In time, people will realize it.

You will earn their respect.

Couldn't anyone find a better word than "dyslexia?"

There are far too many ways to misspell it.

Couldn't they have called it "mixed-uppityness?"

Or even "enhanced misdirection syndrome."

Or "word craziness."

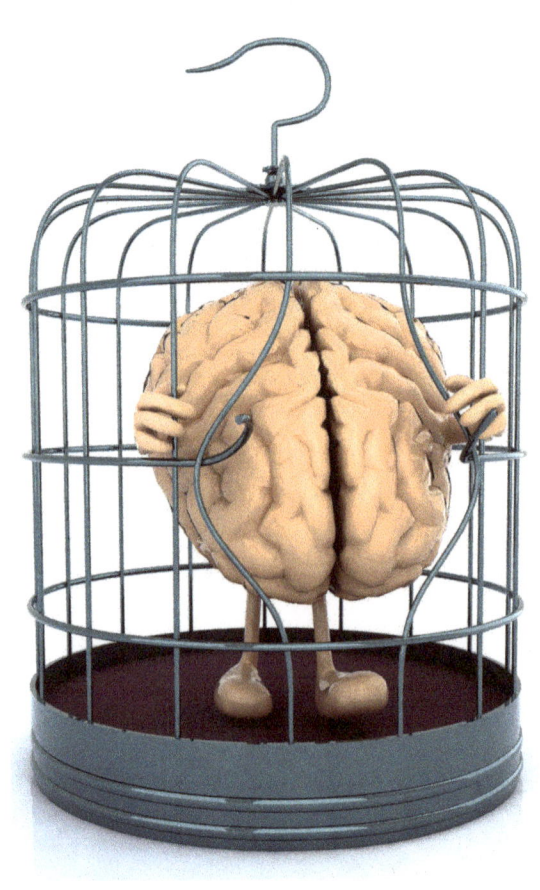

About your brain.

Your brain is fine.

In fact, it's a perfectly good brain, with excellent thoughts going through it.

Sometimes information that goes into the brain gets messed up along the way and comes out weirdly, but look around you.

Everybody's brain makes mistakes.

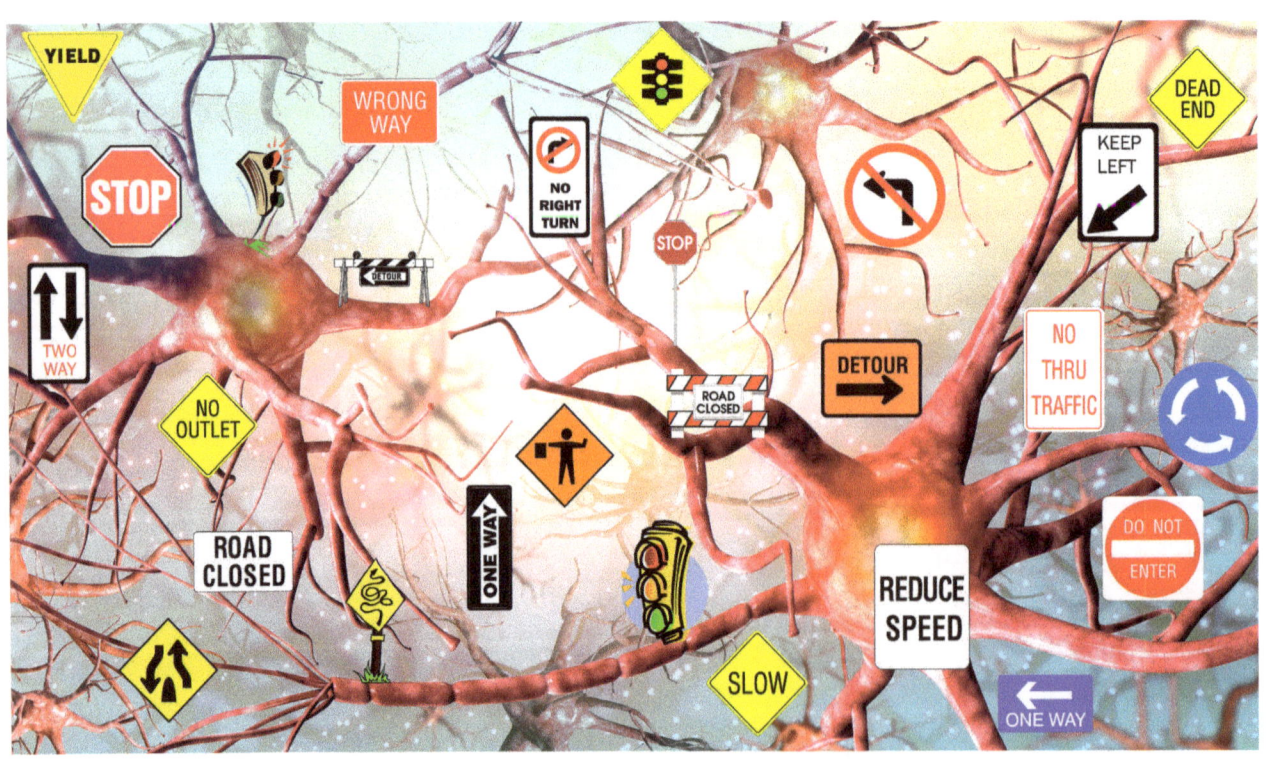

Do thoughts get lost running around in your brain?

Artists and philosophers spend years learning to see the world in new ways.

Dyslexics are born seeing the world differently. Take advantage of it.

Unleash the creative power of your great brain. Turn it loose.

You are not the only one.

About one out of five people are dyslexic.

That's right -- one in five. They're all around you.

One in five.

And, dyslexia sometimes runs in families.

There may be people close to you who can talk to you about it.

By the way, dyslexia is not contagious.

Talk about it.

If you can openly tell people that you have dyslexia, and that you're struggling with one or more particular problems, you will be surprised at how many people will share that they also are dyslexic.

They will probably tell you a story about a dyslexic moment in their lives, and they will want to help you any way they can.

They can't cure you, and they may not even be able to help with your problem of the moment, but they've found ways to cope with dyslexia. You can, too.

Having someone you know, someone who is functioning "normally," share their own experiences can make a difference because it's proof that dyslexia doesn't win. It can't be "cured," but you can defeat it every day.

Just find your own way.

Problems at School.

If you're dyslexic, you're probably having trouble at school.

When teachers explain things, it seems like they often make them harder.

They use big words when simple words will do.

They talk fast when you're struggling to keep up.

Their answers to your questions are rushed and complicated and just repeat what you didn't understand and just repeat what you didn't understand and just repeat what you didn't understand.

Because dyslexia is the result of difficulty processing sounds, all of these things can cause problems that show up through writing and reading.

How can you deal with those problems?

1. Ask for help.
2. Work hard.
3. Repeat.

The thing that some kids dread most of all is reading out loud in front of their classmates. It's hard to think straight when your mind is racing and your thoughts are crashing against the inside of your skull. Relax. You'll be fine.

There are too many stories of kids who would rather act up and get thrown out of class than be embarrassed by making mistakes in front of their classmates.

Don't be that kid. Talk to your teacher. Ask for help.

Reading is hard.

So you don't like to read, but everyone makes you read anyway.

Get used to it.

Admit it. Some of those books have good stuff in them. Whatever you're interested in, there are books about it.

So, make sure you get the good books. Ask around.

There are gazillions of books to choose from. (You don't have to read them all.)

Even if reading is hard, read anyway. Don't let a book beat you. It's okay to read slowly. It's okay to read something more than once. It's okay to have someone read to you, or to listen to a recording of a book.

Nobody will tell you this, but if you're reading a book that you don't like -- close it. Put it aside. Try a different book. And another.

Someday, maybe you'll go back to the book you put aside. Maybe it'll be better then. That happens.

Some books you have to be ready for.

Writing is hard.

Perfectly good thoughts can be expressed in odd ways and are not clearly understood by your reader.

Don't worry about the words and how they are supposed to go together. Concentrate on your imagination. Express your thoughts.

But be smart -- use spell check.

And read it again before you turn it in. Have someone else look over your writing. They may find errors that you didn't see.

Math is hard.

That doesn't mean you can't do it. You may need more time. You may need things to be explained more than once. That's okay.

Most teachers know more than one way to explain math problems and you may need a completely different explanation than the rest of your class. Keep asking questions.

Check your work. Have someone else look over your assignments. They may find mistakes you didn't notice.

What does a test feel like to a dyslexic student?

1. Explain how de whalluperstm and gllllll-restlb compare. _____

2. List the reasons tha scorbobble frnchullest in the republagle. Show your wrok.

3. YOU'RE OUT OF TIME! PASS YOUR TEST TO THE FRONT!

4. Giw many fo ther woxhengles sutablex gorwhicky gflumph?

5. Name the sltplesness and formgalagle of dglclpr.

6. Filb in da balannnk_____ and _____.

7. Choose anzwer C. below.
    a. Rong.
    b. Stell wrongg.
    d. Wrang agun.

8. _____ and _____ go here.

9. Rratte stuff u dinnat understnad heer. _____
   _____

10. Y R U lazy? _____
    _____

Trouble at home.

When there are problems in school, there is usually trouble at home, too

About your parents.

You have to help them understand.

Don't give up on them. They mean well.

Keep trying. It doesn't get easy, but it gets easier.

Note to parents: Don't you give up either. Think about what it feels like to be a kid with this problem. Get your kid some help.

There are tests that diagnose dyslexia. You won't need to study for them and you can't fail them.

If they find that you have dyslexia, you have certain rights that mean you can get help. That is the law.

You'll learn compensation strategies. Some people call them workarounds. They are simply ways to get around whatever problem you're struggling with. Break the rules.

You're having trouble in school with letters, so whatever grades the teacher puts on your report card, tell your parents that what you see are "A's."

And stick to your story.

What can you do?

Work hard.

That's it. That's what you can do. It may be hard, but people will notice -- and that's good.

They will be impressed. You'll get help. Things will get better and better.

Technology can help.

Sometimes it's easier to type than to write with a pen or pencil.

There are apps that can read text aloud to you.

You can dictate to software that will type your words.

There are special fonts for your computer that may help you. (Like this one: OpenDyslexic 3.)

You can record your thoughts into a recorder.

There are pens that record a teacher's lecture as you write notes.

You are not lazy.

Ask for help.

Everyone else does. And you deserve an equal chance.

Ask for bigger print on the things you need to read.

Ask for more time to read your assignment or take your tests.

Ask for things to be read aloud to you. Or for audio books. Ask if you can record class lectures and listen to them later.

Ask for oral exams or large print tests.

Maybe you just need a break to calm down. Or a hug.

Ask if you can take a walk.

Maybe you need a quiet room. Or maybe you need loud music.

Maybe you need to run off some steam, to get your energy level down to where you can concentrate.

Maybe you need a beer (just kidding). That's for later.

Don't wait until you need the help. Ask early and often.

Start with your parents. Have them talk to your teachers ahead of time -- before you fall behind.

Getting help.

There are answers. Some of them are hidden.

Ask around. Look it up. Try different things. Go to the library (books again!). Search the Internet. Watch videos. Find a support group. Learn about disability programs at your school. There are even conferences that are all about dyslexia. Talk to your parents (again). Ask your teachers (again).

When people tell you stories about their dyslexic moments, they're saying they want to help. They know what it's like and they're doing fine, even if it's hard.

From time to time, you're going to make a silly mistake. So laugh. If you can laugh at your mistakes, it can make them less important and take away the pain.

Music can help.

Some people like to make music. Some just like to listen.

Maybe music will relax you. There are people who believe it changes the way we think.

Some people find that reading music is easier than reading words. Try it.

You probably know lots of songs. If you're having trouble remembering something for school, make up a song about it.

Reading is not the most important thing in the world.

Neither is spelling.   And neither is math.

Life may be a test, but it's not a math test.

Maybe you're good with your hands.

Maybe you're artistic.

Maybe you're a good listener. We need more of those.

Maybe you're good with mechanical things.

Maybe you're good at sports.

Maybe you're musical.

Maybe you're good with people.

Maybe you're good with kids (who are also people).

Maybe you just need a nap.

If you think differently, maybe you look at things differently, too.

You see things in a way that most people don't.

So maybe you'll see a different way to solve a problem.

That happens a lot.

Take action.

Don't sit around waiting for something or someone to solve your problems.

You're in charge. Get creative. Show off a little.

If you don't like reading books, write a book. Write one that you would like to read. (It can be short.)

Graphic novels are books, too. Reading them counts. So does writing and drawing them.

Build something. Make it out of wood or paper or plastic or cookie dough.

Make it roll or fly or glow. Call it an invention or a sculpture or a paperweight.

Try something new. Can you sew or cook or paint? Make some mistakes.

Make a map. Take something apart (check with your parents first). Try a new language. Start a club.

Run for office. Help someone keep a secret. Learn a magic trick. Make a funny sign.

Write a poem that only you will understand. Make it into a snog -- er, a song. Or a snog.

After school.

Yes, someday it will all be over.

Once you're out of school, the tests stop.

There's nothing you can't do.

Except maybe reading.

And writing.

And spelling.

And math.

Why is that not a problem? Simple...

For reading, you'll listen to audio books or watch videos.

For writing, you'll dictate, either to a person or a recorder or a computer.

For spelling, you'll use a Spell Check app -- or an editor.

For math, you'll use a calculator or a computer or you'll find an accountant.

You're going to be happy.

Time management.

Time. There's not enough of it. That's true for everyone, but it's even more true for a dyslexic person taking a test.

Time management skills can be developed. That means don't put things off, even when you want to. Get organized. Make a schedule. Take notes.

Start early, take breaks when you need them, then get back to work. Finish.

Waste time well.

Daydreaming is just another word for thinking.

Imagination and creativity can be hard work. Take credit for it. Explore your thoughts and ideas. Talk about them with others.

Try new things. Make mistakes. Maybe even get in trouble (not too much trouble, but experimentation can have consequences).

Find something you like to do and become really good at it. Then teach someone how to do it.

Laugh a lot. Never be embarrassed. Be proud.

Get a job.

People with dyslexia have lots of different jobs. Some may be a better match for you than others.

You've got plenty of time, but think ahead. What are you good at? What do you enjoy? What are your strengths? What do you want to be?

For example, it may surprise you to learn that dyslexic people do all of these jobs (so pick one): paleontologist, coach, president, teacher, governor, athlete, architect, guitarist, engineer, race driver, soldier, neuroscientist, designer, doctor, general, attorney, inventor, comedian, biophysicist, astronaut, mathematician, poet, wrestler, entrepreneur, senator, cartoonist, and lots more.

You probably won't be an air traffic controller, or if you become one, you'll probably want to keep your mouth shut about being dyslexic.

Maybe proofreading isn't going to be your thing.

Maybe you'll talk for a living instead -- like a salesman, or a minister, or a radio personality, or a politician.

Maybe the patience you've learned will let you help others. Maybe you'll be a teacher or a caregiver.

Maybe you'll be a writer or an actor or a singer or a filmmaker or an artist (but probably not a tattoo artist).

And maybe you'll be a parent.

Famous dyslexic successes.

You've probably seen lists of people who are dyslexic and became successful.

Here are some famous examples: Leonardo da Vinci, Walt Disney, Albert Einstein, Alexander Graham Bell, Nikola Tesla, F. Scott Fitzgerald, John Lennon, Pablo Picasso, Mohammed Ali, Babe Ruth, Henry Ford, Thomas Edison, Agatha Christie, Steve Jobs, Ben Franklin, Robin Williams, Winston Churchill, Lewis Carroll, Thomas Jefferson, Hans Christian Andersen, W.B. Yeats, Galileo Galilei, Jules Verne, George Patton, John F. Kennedy, and George Washington. What a bunch of showoffs!

No one really knows if they were all dyslexic or not. Many of them died before dyslexia was even invented.

Christopher Columbus went West to find the East, so maybe he was dyslexic. Tarzan was a poor reader. What about him? Or Santa Claus, who never quite brings you what you asked for? Moses was lost for forty years, so he was probably dyslexic. The Tyrannosaurus Rex is extinct. Did dsylexia get 'em?

Don't worry about being famous. Just know that success comes in a zillion different ways. You'll find your own path and make your own list.

Be proud.

Let everyone know there's a smart person inside of you.

How do you do that? Open your mouth and let your words out. Tell them your great ideas.

Or, show them what you can do.

Life isn't just reading and writing and math -- thank goodness. It's about personality and perseverance and how you are with others.

And hard work. Keep at it.

There's going to be a happy ending.

None of these problems matter. It may not seem like it now, but you're going to be fine.

Also -- you just finished reading a book. Keep it up.

THE BEGINNING

ABOUT THE AUTHER

Jimmy Huston proudly holds a nonexistent degree in Dyslexiology from the University of REDACTED.

He is also a founding member of the Secret Order of Dyslexia, but won't admit it.

And, he holds the collegiate record for the most unforced typographical errors in a single word.

He lives in Woodland Hills, California, where he devotes his time to laboratory research working toward an inexpensive vaccine for dyslexia.

www,byjimmyhuston.com

Other Books by Jimmy Huston

www.cosworthpublishing.com

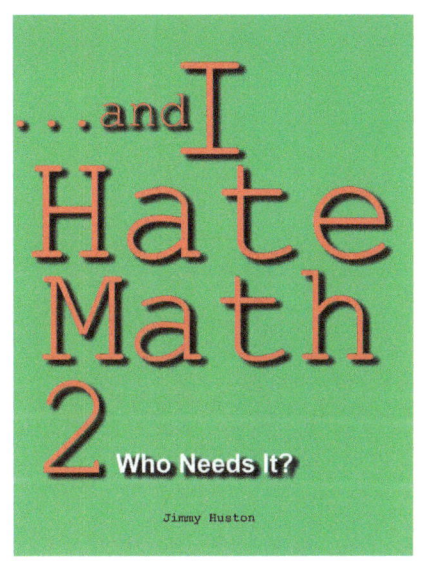

Find it wherever good books are dreaded.

If you're reading this, you will not like this book. It's not for you.

This book is for all the people who are *not* reading this.

They won't like it either, but it's short.

They'll like that.

"I didn't actually read this book. If I had, I would have loved it — but I never will."
— Billy

"'Hate' isn't a strong enough word for me. I loathe reading. I don't even like looking at pictures — which there are none of."
— Wally

"This isn't what I wrote about this stupid book."
— Zane

"This is an excellent coffee table book, if your coffee table hates to read."
— Solomon

"This book made my teacher cry."
— David

"My son loved this book. He said it was delicious."
— Mr. Jones

"THIS BOOK IS SO DUMB THAT I COULD'VE WRITTEN IT."
— Jimmy

www.i-hate-to-read.com

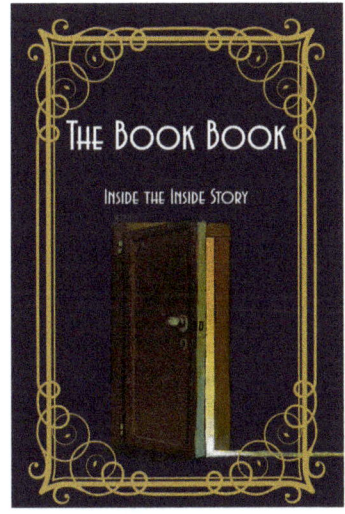
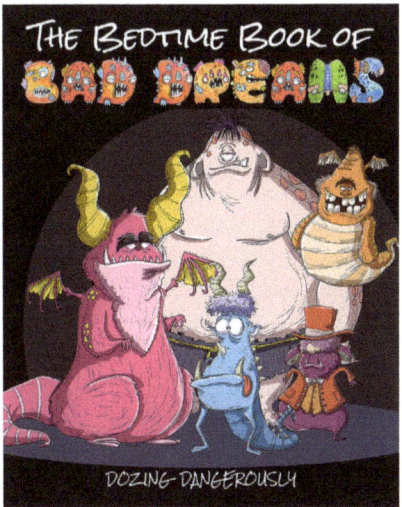

More Books from Jimmy Huston

www.cosworthpublishing.com

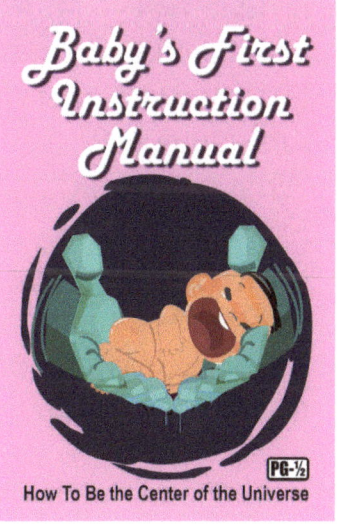

Dead Is the New Sick
An Insider's Guide to Senility, Paranoia, & Curmudgery

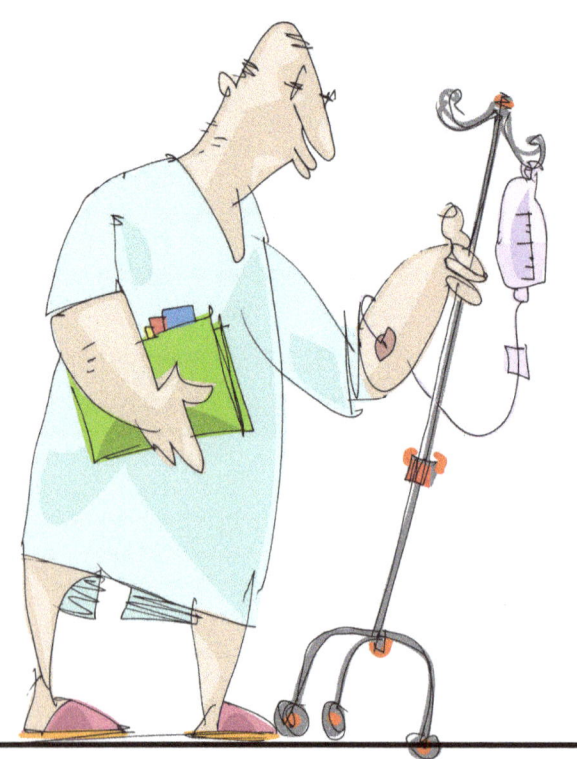

"Warmly affectionate elder abuse."
— Methuselah

"Sadly funny..."
— Sophocles

"The Pet Rock of western literature."
— Anon.

"I don't feel so good."
— John Doe

Top 10 Warnings

1. Hospice is a crock. Keep a jug of water under the bed.
2. Write a will.
4. Hide it.
5. Don't walk toward the light.
6. Did you take your meds today?
7. Are you sure?
8. What happened to Number 3?
9. Eat a pie.
10. If there has ever been something you wanted to do, but didn't for whatever reason, now is the time to do it! Start with this book!

www.deadsick.com

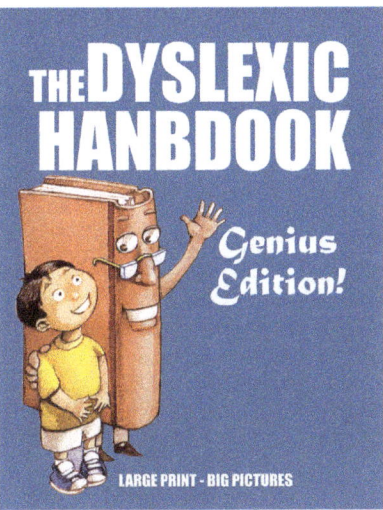

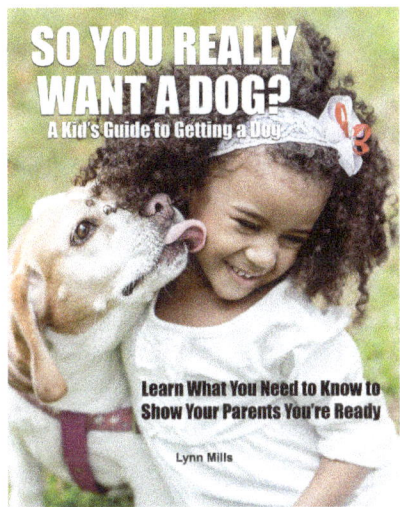

More Books from Cosworth Publishing
www.cosworthpublishing.com

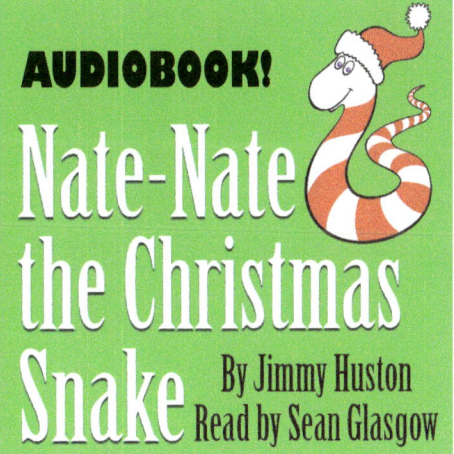

Books for Grownups from Cosworth Publishing
www.cosworthpublishing.com

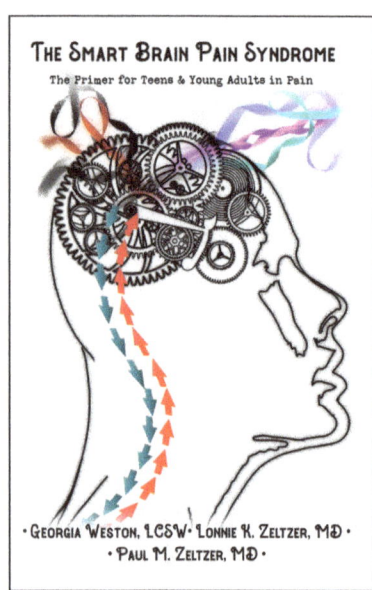

A groundbreaking new book. Three experts explain chronic pain to teens and parents, including using creative outlets to displace the pain.

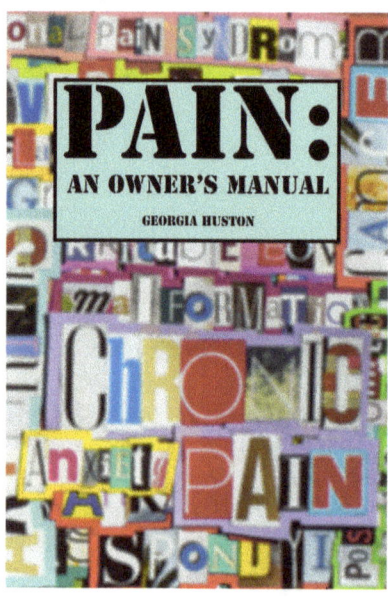

A young pain victim's inspirational and informative conversations with a variety of pain sufferers and specialists. Doctors should read this at their own risk.

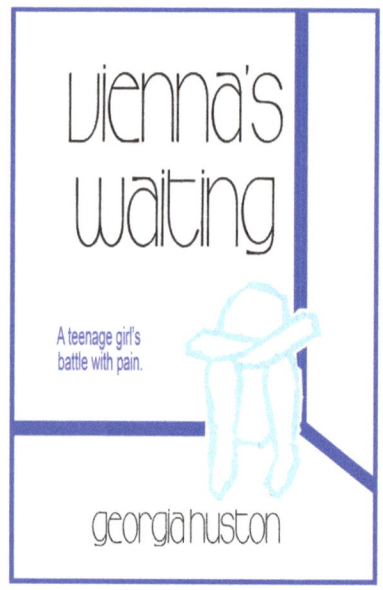

At 14, Georgia developed mysterious chronic pain. This book chronicles that dark time and follows her inspirational journey back to health and happiness.

A practical guide for the person who is confronted by the possible suicide of a friend or family member.

A young Jewish scribe flees WWII Europe with his in-progress Torah, escaping into China under Japanese occupation.

AUDIOBOOK

A powerful reading of Georgia's harrowing experiences as a young teen suffering chronic pain. Hearing it all out loud brings new power and meaning to this true-life story.

One of the very best new books about Christmas and reptiles!

Ripped from the headlines of Candy Cane Lane!

Follow little Nate-Nate as he explores Candy Cane Lane on Christmas Eve. He is not exactly welcomed by the neighborhood, but through his adventures Nate-Nate discovers the spirit of Christmas despite being a lowly snake in everyone's eyes.

When the joyful holiday mood is threatened, he slithers to the rescue and becomes the legend known far and wide as Nate-Nate the Christmas Snake.

No snakes were harmed in the writing of this book.

**NOW AVAILABLE AS AN AUDIOBOOK FROM AUDIBLE.COM
Read by Sean Philip Glasgow**

www.christmassnake.com

Thanks for buying, borrowing, or swiping this wonderful book.

At Cosworth Publishing we truly appreciate that, and in return, we'd like to offer you one of our E-books absolutely free—and worth every penny.

Just let us know that you want it, and we'll make sure that you get it. Let us know which book you read so we don't send you the same one.

Send an email to *office@cosworthpublishing.com*.

Then, from time to time, we will let you know via email when we have a new book that you might be interested in.

We won't do that very often because we're basically pretty lazy, and we don't produce very many new books.

Reviews are usually appreciated.

www.ingramcontent.com/pod-product-compliance
Lightning Source LLC
Chambersburg PA
CBHW040003080526
44586CB00027B/2869